714

MATH
ON THE JOB

Working in Construction

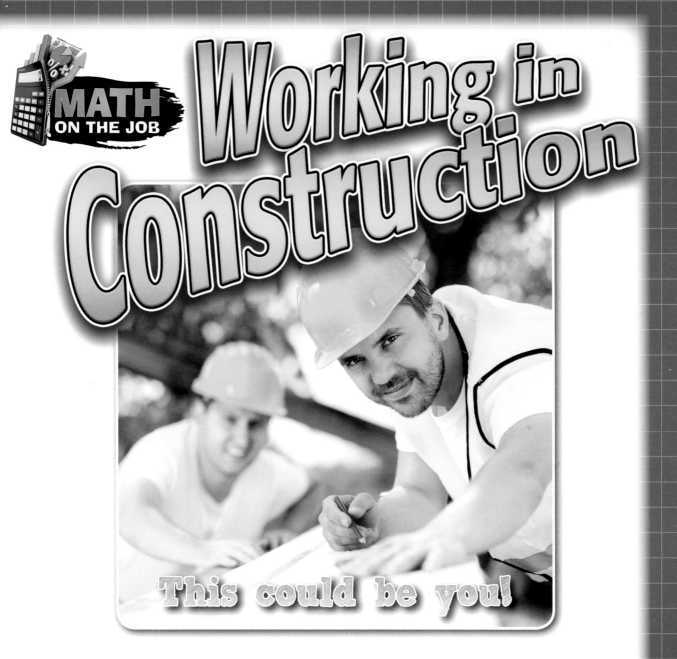

This could be you!

Rick Wunderlich

Crabtree Publishing Company
www.crabtreebooks.com

D1223666

Crabtree Publishing Company
www.crabtreebooks.com

Dedicated by Rick Wunderlich
To my daughter Mary, a wonderful daughter and superb mother.

Author: Rick Wunderlich

Editorial director: Kathy Middleton

Editors: Reagan Miller, Janine Deschenes, and
Kathy Middleton

Proofreader: Crystal Sikkens

Photo research: Margaret Amy Salter

Designer: Margaret Amy Salter

Production coordinator and prepress technician:
Margaret Amy Salter

Print coordinator: Katherine Berti

Math Consultant: Diane Dakers

All images by Shutterstock

Special thanks to Elijah Hansen

Library and Archives Canada Cataloguing in Publication

Wunderlich, Rick, author
    Math on the job : working in construction / Richard Wunderlich.

(Math on the job)
Includes index.
Issued in print and electronic formats.
ISBN 978-0-7787-2361-5 (bound).--
ISBN 978-0-7787-2369-1 (paperback).--
ISBN 978-1-4271-1742-7 (html)

    1. Construction industry--Mathematics--Juvenile literature.
2. Mathematics--Juvenile literature. I. Title. II. Title: Working in
construction.

TH149.W86 2016   j510.2'4624   C2015-908046-0
                                             C2015-908047-9

Library of Congress Cataloging-in-Publication Data

CIP available at the Library of Congress

Crabtree Publishing Company
www.crabtreebooks.com   1-800-387-7650

Printed in Canada/022016/IH20151223

Published in Canada
Crabtree Publishing
616 Welland Ave.
St. Catharines, ON
L2M 5V6

Published in the United States
Crabtree Publishing
PMB 59051
350 Fifth Avenue, 59th Floor
New York, New York 10118

Published in the United Kingdom
Crabtree Publishing
Maritime House
Basin Road North, Hove
BN41 1WR

Published in Australia
Crabtree Publishing
3 Charles Street
Coburg North
VIC 3058

Contents

Please note:
The standard and metric systems are used interchangeably throughout this book.

Construction Workers

Construction worker is a general term used to describe a person working in any career involved in the design, planning, building, and repairing of homes, buildings, bridges, and other structures. Carpenters, crane operators, and electricians are different kinds of construction workers.

Imagine you are an **apprentice** in construction work. An apprentice is someone learning the skills of a particular job from a skilled worker. Perhaps you want to be a carpenter. Imagine using your skills to help build someone a new games room where they can play video games or enjoy other fun activities.

Maybe you'd rather become a construction worker who **operates** the giant crane that lifts massive machinery to the tops of skyscapers. Or what about becoming an electrician? Imagine your job is to **install** electric wiring into new apartments. Can you see yourself working in these careers? This could be you!

Whether you are a carpenter, a crane operator, or an electrician, imagine the satisfaction of returning to the homes, schools, or skyscrapers you worked on after they are finished, and being able to say to people, "I helped build that!"

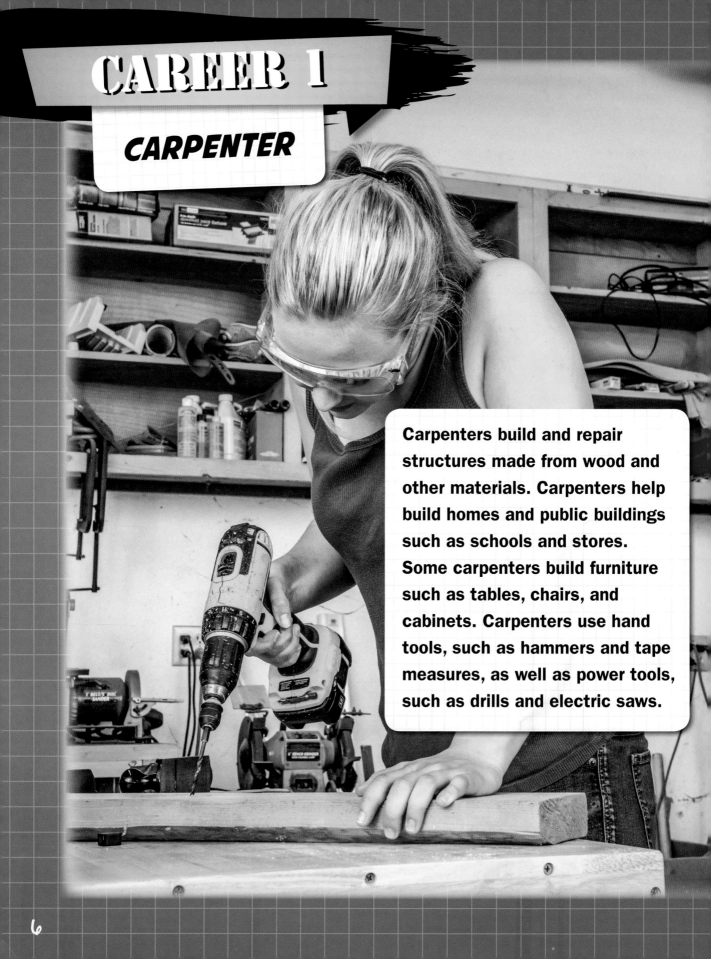

CAREER 1

CARPENTER

Carpenters build and repair structures made from wood and other materials. Carpenters help build homes and public buildings such as schools and stores. Some carpenters build furniture such as tables, chairs, and cabinets. Carpenters use hand tools, such as hammers and tape measures, as well as power tools, such as drills and electric saws.

Think Like a Carpenter

Carpenters need to know how to read **blueprints**. Blueprints are detailed plans that include diagrams, measurements, and instructions for a construction project that builders must follow. It is the job of designers, called architects, to make blueprints for customers such as home builders.

This is a blueprint of a house. It shows the layout and sizes in feet of each room in the design.

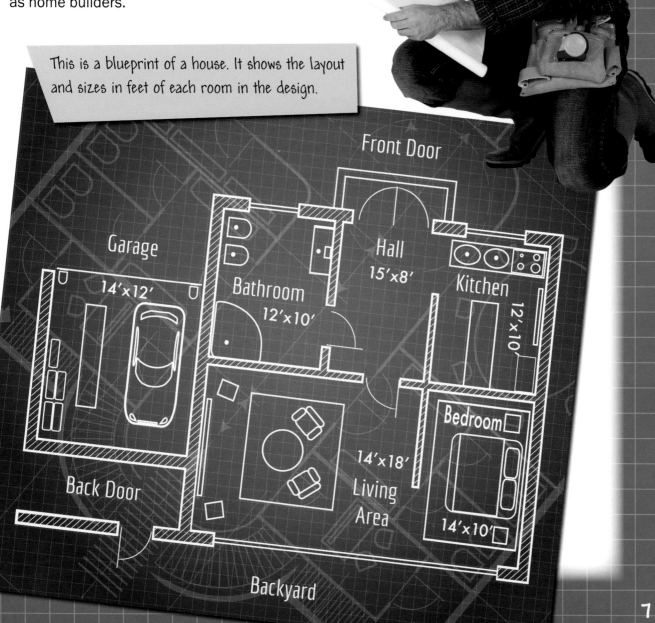

Front Door

Garage

14'x12'

Bathroom
12'x10'

Hall
15'x8'

Kitchen

12'x10'

Bedroom

Back Door

14'x18'
Living
Area

14'x10'

Backyard

Imagine you are working as a carpenter. Your job is to build a games room. This games room is 20 feet long and 15 feet wide. You will be installing oak flooring in the room.

SOLVE:

1 First, you must figure out the area of the floor to be covered. The bigger the floor space, the more expensive it will be for the owner to buy enough oak to cover it. Area is written as square units (in this case, square feet). Use the equation below to figure out the area, in square feet, of the games room floor:

Area of a rectangle = length × width.

2 The flooring is sold in cases of planks, and each case contains 20 square feet of flooring. How many cases will be needed to cover the entire floor area?

3 If the flooring costs $75 per case, what is the total cost of the flooring needed to cover the games room floor?

FACTS:

Sometimes carpenters need to change measurements into different units in order to solve problems. For example, if a carpenter needs to make a 1-foot-wide beam out of 1-inch-wide strips of wood, he needs to know that there are 12 inches in one foot. So, 12 strips will need to be nailed together. Other conversions workers might use are:

3 feet = 1 yard	1 ton = 2,000 pounds
5,280 feet = 1 mile	1 kilogram = 1,000 grams

CONVERT:

1 Refer to the box on page 9 and use multiplication to complete the conversion table at right:

LARGER UNITS	SMALLER UNITS	
3 feet	_____	inches
100 yards	_____	feet
2 kilograms	_____	grams
5 tons	_____	pounds
1/2 mile	_____	feet

CAREERS THAT COUNT

NAME: Elijah Hansen
POSITION: Apprentice Carpenter

How do you use math in your career?

My name is Elijah Hansen. The company that I work for builds waste treatment and water treatment plants (buildings). If you live in a city, when you flush your toilet the water goes into a pipe and carries it to a plant that cleans it. When you turn your faucets on the water comes from a plant that makes that water safe to drink. My company builds those types of plants. As a carpenter, I use math a lot. Having a good understanding of math helps on the job. When we check to make sure that a building is square, we use **trigonometry**. Inches are broken down into 16ths on a standard tape measure. This means that we use fractions a lot at work. Some measurements on blueprints are also written down in tenths of an inch, so we have to convert the tenths into 16ths, and sometimes the 16ths back into tenths.

DECIDE:

Suppose the owner of the house asks you to help her decide if a pool table measuring 8 feet long and 4 feet wide will fit in the games room. She says she wants at least 5 feet of empty space surrounding the pool table so that the players will have room to make their shots. You have to decide if it will fit.

1 Create a diagram of measurements of the room, pool table, and empty space to find out if the pool table will fit. Show the math that supports your answer.

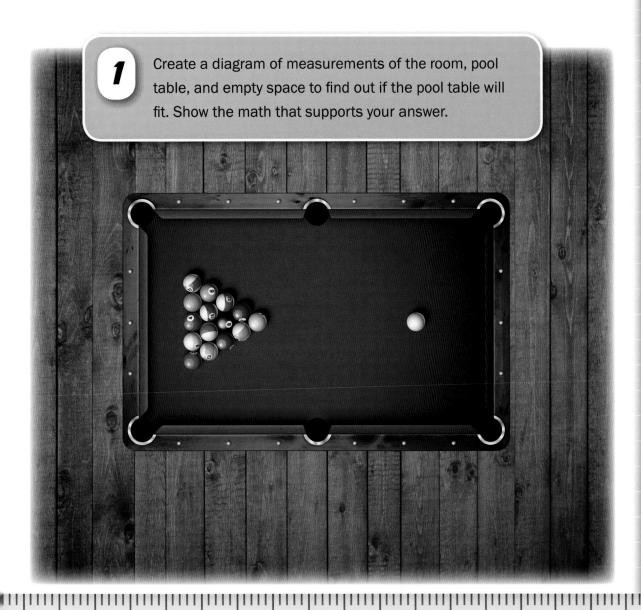

TOUGH DECISION:

Suppose the owner wants you to decrease the room size from 20 feet x 15 feet to 18 feet x 14 feet.

1 By how many square feet does the total area of the room decrease?

2 Does the pool table, with 5 feet of extra space on all sides, fit in the smaller room size, or would you recommend she get a smaller pool table?

MATH
TOOLBOX

CONVERTING MEASUREMENTS

To compare lengths that are measured in both feet and inches, convert the measurements in feet to measurements in inches by multiplying by 12. You multiply by 12 because there are 12 inches in 1 foot.

Imagine you plan to insert a window into a wall. Some of the dimensions of the wood you need to order for the window frame might be in feet and others in inches. For example, one size of lumber often used in building is:

8 feet long x 1.5 inches thick x 3.5 inches wide.

The measurements are in both feet and inches. To make things simpler, a carpenter might convert the feet to inches by multiplying 8 feet x 12 inches. This equals 96 inches.

WANT TO BE A CARPENTER?

1. Stay in school! Learn as much as you can in technical education classes, such as woodworking, and in math classes.

2. Go to your school or local library and ask about vocational schools that offer carpentry programs.

3. Carpenters must be skilled using a variety of tools. You can try simple woodworking projects to start learning the basics. Don't forget to have adult supervision when you are using carpentry tools. They can be very dangerous if proper safety rules are not being followed.

CAREER

PATHWAYS

This could be you!

CAREER 2

CRANE OPERATOR

Crane operators know how to use machines that have long lifting arms and cables to hoist or lower large or heavy objects. They know how to operate them safely, especially around electrical wires, as well as other workers and big machines. Crane operators must also have knowledge of angles, lengths, and weights in order to set up their cranes to lift heavy loads safely.

Materials that are too heavy to be lifted by workers are moved by cranes to where they are needed on construction sites. Cranes are also used to help put together projects such as log homes. Skyscrapers, large ships, and bridges are all built with the help of cranes. They are also used on ships and on docks to load and unload freight, such as new cars. Cranes can also be used to move objects over barriers, such as rivers, without disturbing the river environment.

Crane operators begin as apprentices, learning a great deal on the job from experienced and qualified crane operators. They must also take classes that focus on safety procedures, and wire, rope, and rigging instruction, as well as crane maintenance. Rigging is the work of adjusting the crane's **hoists and pulleys** to make sure oversize loads are securely held and transported.

Think Like a Crane Operator

A load being lifted by a crane needs to be balanced. That means the weight of the load must be even on each side of where it is attached to the crane's cable. Otherwise, it could tilt dangerously and hit something—maybe even the crane!

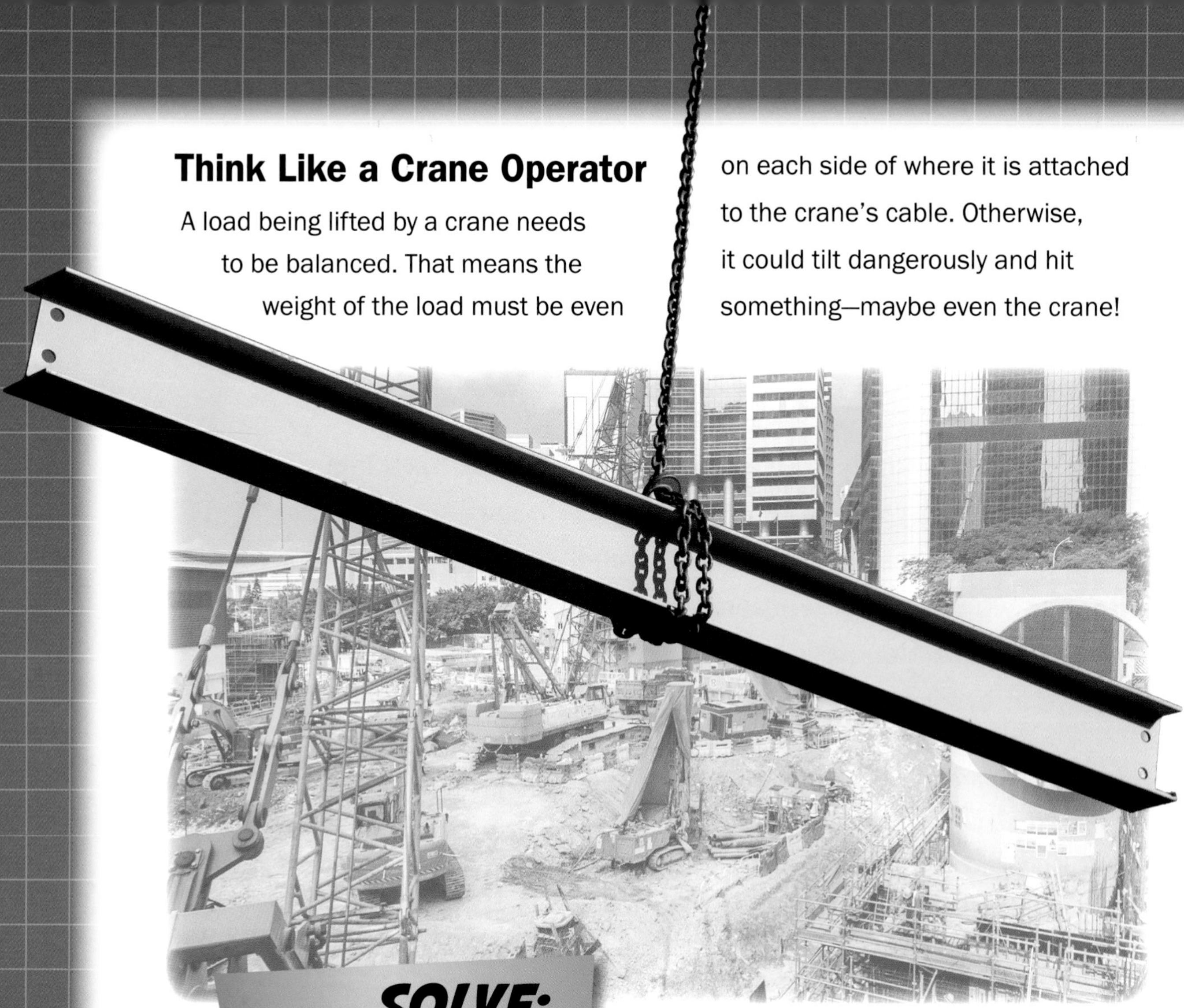

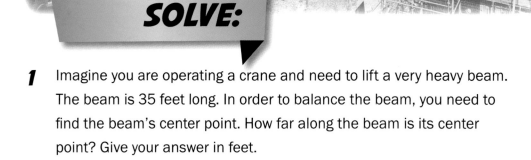

SOLVE:

1 Imagine you are operating a crane and need to lift a very heavy beam. The beam is 35 feet long. In order to balance the beam, you need to find the beam's center point. How far along the beam is its center point? Give your answer in feet.

2 The beam weighs ½ ton. If the crane cable weighs 215 pounds, what is the total weight of the beam plus the cable? Give your answer in pounds. (Refer to page 9 for help converting.)

3 If the maximum load the crane can lift safely is 2,500 pounds, how many tons is that? Can the crane safely lift this load?

A journeyman **rigger is a person trained to set up the system of hoists and pulleys on a crane. A rigger learns how to read and use reference cards that show how to set up a crane to safely carry loads of different weights and sizes. The example below shows the rigger what amount of weight can be safely held by different wire thicknesses, and at what angles the wires can bend.**

Journeyman Rigger's Reference Card

Sling Capacities

MECHANICAL SPLICE IN POUNDS   DESIGN FACTOR   5:1   ①

Size in inches	1.00 VERTICAL	.75 CHOKER	2 - Legs or Basket 90° 2.00	60° 1.73	45° 1.41	30° 1.00	3 - Legs 60° Only if 1/3 each leg 2.60	Size in mm
1/4	1,300	960	2,600	2,200	1,820	1,300	3,300	6.4
5/16	2,000	1,480	4,000	3,400	2,800	2,000	5,100	8.0
3/8	2,800	2,200	5,600	5,000	4,000	2,800	7,400	9.6
7/16	3,800	2,800	7,600	6,800	5,400	3,800	10,000	11.0
1/2	5,000	3,800	10,000	8,800	7,200	5,000	13,200	13.0
9/16	6,400	4,800	12,800	11,000	9,000	6,400	16,500	14.0
5/8	7,800	5,800	15,600	13,600	11,000	7,800	20,000	16.0
3/4	11,200	8,200	22,400	19,400	15,800	11,200	29,100	19.0
7/8	15,200	11,200	30,400	26,000	22,000	15,200	39,000	22.0
1	19,600	14,400	39,200	34,000	28,000	19,600	51,000	25.4
1-1/8	24,000	18,000	48,000	42,000	34,000	24,000	62,000	28.5
1-1/4	30,000	22,500	60,000	52,000	42,000	30,000	76,000	32.0
			MULTIPLIER →	1.00	.75	.60	← MULTIPLIER	

Wire Rope EIPS IWRC

Formula to find sling length Total distance between pick points x Multiplier = Sling Length

A journeyman rigger calculates a load's approximate weight, then uses the information to figure out the safest way to secure and lift the load.

LOAD: STEEL PLATES

PLATE THICKNESS IN INCHES	WEIGHT PER PLATE IN POUNDS
1/8"	8 lbs
1/4"	16 lbs
3/8"	24 lbs
1/2"	_____
5/8"	_____
3/4"	_____
7/8"	56 lbs
1"	64 lbs

ANALYZE:

1 Fill in the missing weight estimations for each plate thickness. (Tip: It will be easier to compare thickness if you change all the fractions to 8^{ths}.)

2 Look at the completed table. Do you see a pattern in the estimates of the weight of the steel plates?

CALCULATE:

Your supervisor asks you to add materials to the load containing the beam and cable (see page 16). Adding materials to the load could save time and get the materials to the workers faster.

1 If the added materials include 708 pounds of bolts, and 2 steel plates that weigh 303 pounds each, what is the total weight in pounds of the added materials?

2 What is the new total weight of the beam and cable, plus the new load?

3 What is the difference between the new weight and the maximum load of 2,500 pounds? Can the crane safely lift this load?

DECIDE:

You show the supervisor your calculations and suggest that the load of bolts is not safe to lift.

1 How would you show the supervisor, using mathematics, the steps you used to calculate whether the new load is safe?

2 If the supervisor wanted you to take up a partial load of bolts so that workers could at least begin installing the beam, what is the weight of the bolts that must be removed?

MATH TOOLBOX

ESTIMATION

Workers often estimate things like weight and length in order to see if it is likely the load will meet construction requirements. However, before decisions are made, it is very important that workers check their work.

The first step in estimating is to make sure the values of objects being compared or added together have the same units of measurement. For example, if the weights of some objects are given in tons and other objects in pounds, divide the amounts in pounds by 2,000 to convert the units to tons. (Remember, 2,000 pounds = 1 ton.)

To round values, look at the last digit on the right of the number. If the final digit is 5 or above, change that digit to 0 and add one to the digit to its left. If the final digit is 4 or below, change that digit to 0 and the digit to its left stays as it is. For example: 4.6 rounds up to 5, and 4.3 rounds down to 4.

Now that all the measurements are in tons, the second step is to round the values in order to make calculations easier. For example, suppose you are adding:

23.1 tons + 11.8 tons + 1,900 pounds.

- 23.1 tons can be rounded to 23 tons
- 11.8 tons can be rounded to 12 tons
- 1,900 pounds ÷ 2,000 = 0.95 tons, which can be rounded to 1 ton

The sum now becomes 23 + 12 + 1
The estimated total becomes 36 tons.

This could be you!

WANT TO BE A CRANE OPERATOR?

1. Go to your school or local library and ask about vocational schools that offer heavy equipment programs.

2. If there is a construction site near your home, you could go with adult supervision to watch from a safe distance to see machines, such as cranes, at work.

3. Try crane simulator games such as:

https://play.google.com/
store/apps/details?id=com.
vg.CraneParkingExtended&hl=en

CAREER
PATHWAYS

ELECTRICIAN

Electricity travels along a circuit**, or path, that starts where the electrical current is produced, such as at a power plant, and ends where the electricity is used, such as in homes and offices.**

Working with electricity can be dangerous. Electricians are trained to work safely and make sure others are not harmed by incorrect wiring.

Electricians make sure that electricity travels correctly and safely along the path from its **source** to its destination. They install and repair wires and other parts through which electricity travels. Some electricians install wiring to bring electricity into buildings. Others may work on repairing the electrical parts of machines in factories.

Think Like an Electrician

Imagine you are working on the construction site of a new apartment building. You need to install wiring for a new apartment. One of your tasks is to find out how much electricity is used by household appliances. With this information you can plan the wiring for the kitchen.

The table below gives some examples of the electrical current that flows through typical household appliances. Electrical currents are measured in units called **amperes**, or **amps**.

APPLIANCE NAME	CURRENT FLOW IN AMPS
toaster	10
electric kettle	12
dishwasher	10
refrigerator	5

If a circuit is overloaded, or has too much current flowing through it, it can start an electrical fire.

When a circuit is overloaded, a **circuit breaker** can detect the problem and shut off the flow of electricity to prevent a fire.

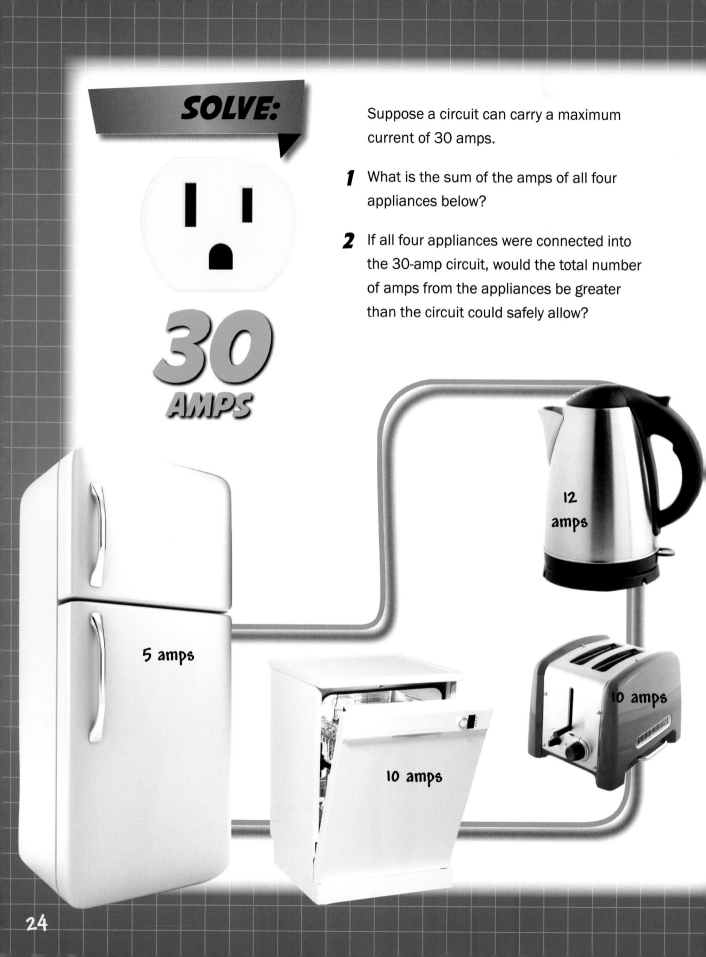

SOLVE:

30 AMPS

Suppose a circuit can carry a maximum current of 30 amps.

1 What is the sum of the amps of all four appliances below?

2 If all four appliances were connected into the 30-amp circuit, would the total number of amps from the appliances be greater than the circuit could safely allow?

12 amps

5 amps

10 amps

10 amps

ammeter

Amperes, or amps, are one of the measures of electrical flow. The higher the amperage in the circuit, the more electricity is able to flow, and the more energy is available for objects that require a high amount of amps such as electric saws.

Electricians must ensure that the electricity flowing through a circuit is not too much. If it is, a fire can result. An electrician can measure the number of amps flowing through a circuit by using an instrument called an ammeter.

Other units used by electricians to measure electricity are volts, which are a measure of electrical force, and watts, which are a measure of the amount of energy used by a circuit. Electricians use this formula that relates all three units:

$$Watts = volts \times amps$$

This means that in a typical household circuit that uses 120 volts, a 10-amp appliance uses 1,200 watts of energy.

ANALYZE:

APPLIANCE	WATTS	VOLTS	AMPS
toaster	1,200	120	10
kettle	____	120	12
dishwasher	____	120	10
refrigerator	____	120	5

1 If a circuit has a breaker that stops electricity flow over 30 amps, list three household appliances from the chart at right that could be turned on at the same time without activating the circuit breaker and cutting off the supply of power to that circuit.

2 Using the formula above, complete the following table that relates watts, volts, and amps. The first one is done for you.

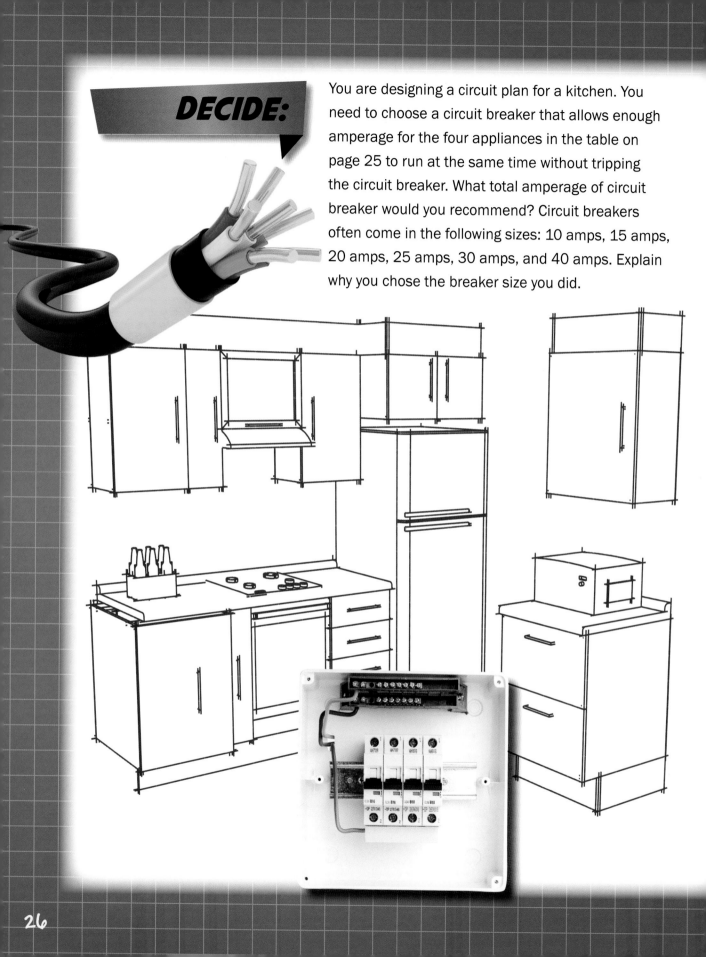

DECIDE:

You are designing a circuit plan for a kitchen. You need to choose a circuit breaker that allows enough amperage for the four appliances in the table on page 25 to run at the same time without tripping the circuit breaker. What total amperage of circuit breaker would you recommend? Circuit breakers often come in the following sizes: 10 amps, 15 amps, 20 amps, 25 amps, 30 amps, and 40 amps. Explain why you chose the breaker size you did.

TOUGH DECISION:

Your supervisor wants you to find the cost of electrical wiring for the kitchen. You draw a diagram of the room and use it to plan the path the electrical wires will follow. The diagram helps you to determine where the wire will go and the length of wire needed. You estimate that the room will require about $20 to $25 worth of wire, including the connectors and **fittings**. You also estimate that it will take between 2 to 2 ½ hours to install the wiring.

1 If one electrician charges $53 per hour plus the cost of materials, and another electrician charges $91 per hour plus the cost of materials, what are the lowest and highest possible total estimates for the wiring job?

2 An electrician goes through stages in their education. Everyone begins as an apprentice, then becomes a journeyman electrician, then may go on to meet the requirements of a master electrician. The more education an electrician has, the more money he or she can charge per hour. This is because electricians with more technical education are able to do more skilled work.

a) If a job takes 2 ½ hours, what is the difference in cost between hiring an electrician who earns $53 per hour and one who earns $91 per hour?

b) Why might a construction company hire a more highly-paid electrician?

AMPS, VOLTS, AND WATTS

Electricians need to learn how to use formulas such as:

amps = watts ÷ volts,
watts = volts × amps.

Electricians use special calculators designed specifically for electrical calculations. Like crane operators, electricians also use reference cards to remind them how to use formulas needed on the job. For example, a customer choosing appliances for his new apartment might ask an electrician about the amount of energy an appliance needs to run.
The electrician could use the formula on a card to estimate the number of watts of energy each appliance would use.

To use these formulas, you substitute the appropriate numbers for the words in the equation, then do the calculation.

Calculation
amps = watts ÷ volts

If watts = 6, and volts = 2:
amps = 6 ÷ 2
amps = 3

Calculation
watts = volts x amps

If volts = 12, and amps = 6:
watts = 12 x 6
watts = 72

WANT TO BE AN ELECTRICIAN?

1. Take a pre-apprenticeship program in high school or at a college.

2. Some schools offer math courses specifically made for students who plan on training for a trade.

3. Ask an electrician questions about his or her work. For example, ask what things they like about their career.

CAREER PATHWAYS

This could be you!

Learning More

Websites

This Math Central link from the University of Regina explores how math is used in construction and design:

http://mathcentral.uregina.ca/beyond/articles/Architecture/ConstructionANDDesign.html

This site provides a great introduction to different careers in construction and explains the skills and education needed for different fields:

www.careersinconstruction.ca

This link gives an overview of a career in carpentry. Information includes the skills and training needed, different work environments, and the outlook for future jobs in the field:

www.bls.gov/ooh/construction-and-extraction/carpenters.htm#tab-1

Books

Robinson, Nancy. *Heavy Equipment Operator*. Cool Careers Series: Cherry Lake Publishing Company, 2011.

Senker, Cath. *Construction Careers*. In the Workplace Series: Amicus Publishing, 2010

Teitelbaum, Michael. *Electrician*. Cool Careers Series: Cherry Lake Publishing Company, 2011.

Answers

Career 1: Carpenter

Solve: 1. The area of the floor is 20 × 15 = 300 square feet.

2. The number of cases of flooring need is 300 ÷ 20 = 15 cases.

3. The cost of the flooring is 15 × $75 = $1,125.

Convert: The numbers needed to fill in the table are: 36 inches, 300 feet, 2,000 grams, 10,000 pounds, 2,640 feet

Decide: 1. Table + extra space: Length 8 + 5 + 5 = 18 feet; Width 4 + 5 + 5 = 14 feet. The pool table with empty spaces on all sides measures 18 ft x 14 ft, which will fit into the room that is 20 feet x 15 feet.

Tough Decision 1. The room has decreased by 300 - 252 = 48 square feet.

2. The 18-foot x 14-foot space needed for the pool table, with extra spaces, will fit exactly.

Glossary

ammeter An instrument that measures the number of amperes flowing through an electrical circuit

amperes/amps The unit of electrical current, often shortened to amp(s)

apprentice A person learning the skills of a particular job from a skilled worker

blueprints A drawing usually showing how something can be put together or constructed

circuit In electricity, the path that electrical energy can follow

circuit breaker A device that interrupts electric flow when the current running through it becomes too great

electrical flow The movement of electricity

estimate To approximate by rounding

fittings Small parts or attachments

hoists and pulleys A system of steel cables around grooved wheels used to raise, lower, or move a load

install To set up to use

journeyman A person who has served an apprenticeship at a trade and is certified to do specific work

operates To cause to work

source A point where something begins

trade A job that requires physical work or skill with machinery

trigonometry A branch of mathematics concerned with the characteristics of triangles

vocational A vocational education is one that prepares students for a trade.

volts A measure of electrical force

watts A measure of the amount of energy used by a circuit

Answers—continued

Career 2: Crane Operator

Solve: 1. The center of the beam is 35 ÷ 2 = 17.5 feet from either end of the beam.

2. The total weight of the beam and cable is $(1/2 \times 2,000) + 215 = 1,215$ pounds.

3. The weight is 2,500 ÷ 2,000 = 1.25 tons. Yes, the crane can lift the load safely.

Analyze: 1. $1/2$" = 32 lbs; $5/8$" = 40 lbs; $3/4$" = 48 lbs

2. Pattern: The weight increases by 8 pounds for every $1/8$" of thickness.

Calculate: 1. The added weight is 708 +303 + 303 = 1,314 pounds.

2. The total weight of beam, cable plus added weight is 1,215 + 1314 = 2,529 pounds.

3. The difference in weight is 2,529 - 2,500 = 29 pounds over the maximum.

The crane cannot safely lift this weight.

Index

Answers—continued

Career 2: Crane Operator

Tough Decision 1. See calculations on page 31 which show mathematical steps taken.

    2. The amount of weight of bolts that must be removed to meet the safety requirement is 2,529 - 2,500 = 29 pounds

Career 3: Electrician

Solve: 1. The sum of the current used by four appliances is 10 + 12 + 10 + 5 = 37 amps.

    2. Yes, the sum of the currents is 7 greater than the 30-amp limit allowed by the circuit breaker.

Analyze: 1. Answers can be any of the following because they total less than 30 amps:
- kettle, dishwasher, and fridge (total 27 amps)
- toaster, kettle, and fridge (total 27 amps)
- toaster, dishwasher, and fridge (total 25 amps)

    2. The missing entries in the table are:

kettle = 120 volts × 12 amps = 1,440 watts,

dishwasher = 120 volts × 10 amps = 1,200 watts,

and refrigerator = 120 volts × 5 amps = 600 watts.

Decide: 1. A 40-amp breaker would work, because the appliances use a total of 37 amps.

Tough Decision:

    1. The lowest cost is $20 + ($53 × 2 hours) = $126.00. The highest cost is $25 + ($91 x 2.5 hours) = $252.50.

    2. a) $53 x 2.5 = $132.50, $91 x 2.5 = $227.50, $227.50-$132.50 = $95 difference in cost

      b) A company might pay more for an electrician if the job requires someone with greater skills.

Author's Bio:

Rick Wunderlich secretly wishes he could try driving heavy equipment like a bulldozer. He also loves playing with toys and can make excellent bulldozer sounds for his grandchildren. Rick has written math and science textbooks and has had the best job in the world for him—a teacher.